WRITE
— HIS —
WRONGS

WRITE
— HIS —
WRONGS

FROM HEARTBREAK
TO LOVE NOTES

J. WESLEY

Brooklyn

Horace Harris Jr.
Visit my website at www.writehiswrongs.com

Printed in the United States of America

ISBN 978-0-9971159-0-1

Author's note: The events described in this book are the author's personal thoughts. I have tried to recreate conversations and locales from my memories. Names and details have been changed to protect the privacy of certain individuals. Some identifying characteristics may have been changed to maintain their anonymity.

Cover photograph copyright © 2016 by Deneka Peniston

Cover design by Jeffrey A. Thacker
Book design by Akasha Archer
Edited by Kate Angus and Ashley Jones-Hatcher

Growing up, dad you told me if you wanted to hide anything from me it would be placed in a book. Well, here is another stash spot. Your reverse psychology skills are magic. I learned how to be a man strictly from watching you. One day I will fill your shoes.

....

To my mom who taught me to think of others before speaking. It got me to write. You made me an author.

....

To my little brother who taught me about responsibility and drive simply by being himself. Harris Brothers. This is only the beginning.

....

To my grandma who saw the light in me when I was at my darkest and keeps our family together through the strength of prayer. I put God first because of you.

....

To my family, you are the village that raised me and proved that where you come from is the most important factor in where you are going as long as love and support are given along the way.

CONTENTS

How deep do I fall in love?
I don't know. I keep falling.

—J. WESLEY

If there is a book that you want to read,
but it hasn't been written yet,
you must be the one to write it.
—TONI MORRISON

AUTHOR'S NOTE

Write His Wrongs started nine years ago as my personal escape from reality. Penning thoughts gave me an opportunity to dictate my love story the way I wanted to. My inability to communicate feelings verbally forced me to watch loved ones come and go—some seeking the answers I knew but refused to share. I wanted to say: *I love you, don't go, I confess, I'm sorry,* but didn't. One day while navigating through a deep funk I started to write—expressing on paper the feelings never shared. I hoped every woman affected by my past would read and gain some clarity. It would not be enough but it was a start. I started to write my wrongs.

My words reaching the attention of readers across the world came unexpectedly. This platform gave me an opportunity to use my experiences, growth and hope to offer change. I published online hoping men would learn from my mistakes and not repeat them. I wanted women to listen to the thought process of a man making decisions in relationships. I needed to show them that men do change. Most importantly, I wanted to bridge the communication gap between genders by exposing myself emotionally— negating any notions of feelings being gender specific. Men and women are not as distant as we have been led to believe. I created my first book From Heartbreak to Love Notes to lessen the gap.

INTRODUCTION

I am not the wisest, smartest, or most fit. I get nervous, excited, scared—sometimes all at once. I shut down when hurt because of what will be said if I open up. I am not the best looking, most graceful, or the coolest chap in the room. I cannot teach classes on being an amazing husband or exceptional boyfriend; instead, I hope there are lessons learned after reading this book.

Perhaps I am a decent man fighting wicked impulses or a wicked man wearing a noble mask for so long that I have convinced myself, he is me. In the past, I disguised lust as love because I healed hurt with lust, so all I felt was pain in love. I loved, lost loved ones, lost myself in it, found a way out only to wake up in its chamber again. Far from the model man with textbook words living a picture-perfect life, I am another person seeking to get it right.

Men learn to protect their hearts during the transition from boy to man. Harboring feelings, our defensive mechanism, damages us more than the harm it was created to protect us from. We hurt until it consumes us and become so fixated on pointing fingers that we fail to notice many wounds were self-inflicted. As society continues to marry women with baggage and trust issues, it is my belief that a man's wall, layered by past emotional letdown, is thicker and towers over those created by women.

My walls are difficult to climb and almost impenetrable. It was never a woman's job to prove why she should enter. It was my responsibility to meet her outside.

My doors are open; women, allow these passages to guide you on my journey to betterment. Men, let us drop our guards and welcome them in.

PART ONE

HEARTBREAK

———

A broken heart continues to beat with reason. You are more alive than your emotions lead you to believe. Every beat, even though pain-filled, is a reminder. If you can still feel . . . you can still heal.

WRITE HIS WRONGS

There were few women I pictured tying the knot with; stability served as my noose. The charm used to rope women in, encouraged them to stay. By the time she realized a future was out of the picture, my last leg was escaping through the window. If abrupt goodbyes were criminal, J. Wesley was a fugitive moving too swift to witness offenses. Posters of me sporting a WANTED crown hug house walls from New York to wherever they moved. Many women attracted to the bad boy hated when I behaved like one.

A dream man to some, a wake-up call to more, I unlocked the shells of women with little regard to what they held dear. I navigated uncharted bodies without any want to settle. Over my shoulder is a trail of damaged hearts and their fleeing spirits forced to embark on another soul search. To this day, declarations of, "We could have been . . ." by women who should have been, haunt me.

PRESENTLY ABSENT

If those free of sin should cast the first stone, my pockets—my hands—empty. When judgment day arrives, hear the whispers of a panicked me crouched in a murky corner attempting to make last-minute amends.

I understood her through speech, but conferences between lips grew foreign. When hers communicated how much she loved me, mine failed to translate. Physically present while mentally absent, I heard without listening. Her cries for help were the faint remains of ending echoes. Our bed became her island. Holding me was as simple as grabbing the sand beneath her feet—no matter how tight the grip I would return to the beach.

Tear trails stain places where smiles and dimples once lived. Drowning while attempting to keep this relationship afloat, she swallows her pain and chokes on salted bitter wants for me. One must be careful in caring, because when careless, you will have to care more. She struggles to hold on because I am fighting to let go.

LOVE TRAP

Broken crayons color,
but broken wings cannot fly.
She, the caged flight seeker,
sings melodic freedom
to a master
entertained by the blues.

THE HOLD

Friends with benefits and exclusively dating
are not titles; they are reasons to close the book.

—J. WESLEY

When I asked her to face her fears, she looked directly at me. Losing hold as we battle coming to grips on what we are, the tug of war noticeably takes its toll on her. "Go! Stay! Let's work it out!" Brash words push her away but my arsenal of gentle ones ease her into coming back. She has no interest in seeking better; she wants me to do better. She may waste years waiting for the day I make up my mind.

TWOSOMES

She wants me for her own. To her, something about us is stronger—more important. I love my girlfriend; what is felt for this other woman is more of an aggressive lust.

I cannot tell you how we got here, at times it feels like we belong. My mistress, convinced we are the better couple, will abandon her boyfriend without hesitation. I do not know her as well as her man, she never supported me like my girl; here we lay contemplating tossing it all away.

Am I cheating myself by remaining faithful? I allowed eye candy to create a cavity in my relationship. While I am on my girlfriend's mind another woman is on mine. News of me stepping out would destroy her. To see my woman cry out of hurt is devastating. I would be a hypocrite to join out of guilt. Tonight I am going to end it—but with who?

REBOUNDS

From the look in her eyes, we are making love. From my vantage point, this is sex. Getting me to cum was one thing—getting me to stay is another. Fresh out of a relationship and into the playing field, I am watering seeds hoping something blossoms. Sleeping with another to get over the other opens up more wounds than it closes; apologies cannot stitch the aftermath.

As I make my way to the door she kisses me goodbye. I kiss her farewell. I was not raised to behave like this. I am better off alone. I keep falling into sheets, but I am not falling in love.

POTENTIAL

W̲e kiss hope, sweat frustration, and make love to a skewed belief that beyond this mattress is the couple of yesteryears. Everything around us screams, **we are not working!** My still heart whispers, *you are the one.*

Accepting no one is perfect is both our saving grace and ruin. The second chances never stopped at two. Wedged between yesterday and the present, reaching for the one we fell for ends in disappointment. We miss every time. It is impossible to hold potential.

DISJOINTED

Do not throw the right words in her ears and expect her to not catch feelings. I never listen. I am one of many men who pursues sex like lions then turns possum when asked about relationships. My want to commit is erased by a fear of attaching it to the wrong person. I entertained women hoping somewhere along the line feelings for them would heighten. "Let's see where this goes" prolonged the inevitable—it rarely led us anywhere.

When women saw me as marriage material, deep down I knew I was destined to rip. Many stayed longer than they should have, reached deeper than they were supposed to, but there was a break in me no ex could fix. Each one came and left. In time, you outgrow the people who wear you out.

SINGLE YET TAKEN

We have issues to address. With no label on this relationship who do we mail our complaints to? We don't. They remain enveloped, forgotten, and sealed with each kiss. Thus creates the lie—not by words spoken from false lips but in the silencing of truthful tongues. You fear my answer more than your question. It may prove we are on different pages of the same story: the main character to one—honorable mention to the other.

Relationships need a title as much as a child needs a name. Mentally you set boundaries that I was never to journey across. What we have is a faux-relationship. We talk like them, walk like them, but we don't walk with them. If I should wander astray and fault like them, I am wrong like them, and you would hurt like her. While you break down and contemplate breaking up, you will break down again when realizing I was never yours to break up with.

Do I have the right to care or the right to remain silent? If we are friends with benefits, where is the friendship once the benefits run out? Our feelings, conveyed through intercourse, rarely over a dinner course. Relationships are strongest when built from the bottom up, not the top down. They become more challenging once crossing the point of bottoms up with tops down.

If sex without a bigger picture in mind remains an empty canvas, where do I begin to draw the line? We need one another. I need to paint; you crave being seen. With every pose, you model the model you have convinced yourself I want you to be. The truth is, my blues will never paint you a heaven and my water cannot wash the pain away.

PUPPET MASTER

Wait a minute! Come here puppet. Why must we continue to play these games?

Which string do I tug on today? *I love you* always strikes a chord but only has a few threads left. Guilt has the tightest grip; I may receive an apology for something I did wrong. Come here puppet with your invisible strings; I am not ready to let you go.

She took a deep breath before turning towards me and responding.

I gave you everything—even the parts I never knew existed. In your possession I was good enough to touch, not hold; speak towards—not talk with. Release me! If you wish me the best and best does not live in you—let me find my way home! Appreciate me when I am here, not when I am gone. You push, I leave, you tug . . . I am yours. Keep your strings—your lies—your hurt. In time, these wounds will heal. I will figure out what to take for the scars.

She exits.

KARMA

Karma never matched me with a cheater and liar; instead, I married the notion that everyone is deceitful and unfaithful. Insecurity filled my pores faster than love ever could. Every time there was a potential to fall, I ran. I didn't only fear who they were, I was afraid of who I would become, which resulted in this unbending refusal to become vulnerable. I could not risk another guy being the other guy. My ability to love wholeheartedly—now reduced to increments—stripped me of being able to trust. Without it I cannot love. That is not living, but that is Karma.

PARTITIONS

Every time I searched for a love to balance the scales, my side kept hitting the floor. After walking away from friends who became strangers and lovers no longer, I formed walls to protect whatever heart remained. Loneliness became my comfort and guardian.

"Why won't you let me in?" she pleads. "Look around! No one stays here! Eventually, I will watch you go!" I turned my back on her. This wall was too thick for me to see her tears. It was too tall for her to see my fears.

UNWANTED

The one who "got away" is often the one who was pushed away and never returned. At first I was miles beyond any man who came before. She went from surprised to accustomed, lacking to curious—now gone. She left longing for items never had but missed them anyway. The next must give her everything I never could.

The only thing I didn't want to give you was a reason to leave. How many doors did you have to knock on to realize that I am home? You left to find everything I wasn't in the next person. You were there searching for everything I was, in the next person.

Unfortunately, people leave you for the same streets that later have them sprinting to the place they left. She returned to new locks and a door bolted—the only love given from me will be from a distance.

REGRETFULLY YOURS

Lonely—the moment when the person you want most is not around. This room, darker than the mood I'm in is faintly lit as fingers scroll through contacts with no one to contact. You, the one I want to fall asleep on, dream with, and wake up to, are gone. She was my sun—I am a moon eclipsed. Move on? Will I be the same after no longer viewing love the same? Can a broken heart love wholeheartedly?

Driven by fear, I opted to stay parked with you. You would give the green to swiftly turn red and never felt guilty for leaving me at a crossroad. My drive yielded reverse effects; remaining neutral got me nowhere.

Connected, I could feel you before I see you, like a teardrop from the eye. My difficulty letting go was because deep down I believed I was not supposed to. I swore the pain felt when walking away was the outstretched arm of my soul not wanting to leave. I long for your touch and have you wrapped in thought; every time I lick the place we kissed, I remember.

MIRAGE

Love had me believing
the one who destroyed me
was the only one capable of repair.
The one I broke up with
is not the one I fell for.
When sharing I miss you,
I have to choose between two
to direct it to.

SILENT NOISE

Fading relationships
will have one believe
numbness cures pain.
Not true.
The hurt is alive and well,
we are,
too exhausted to yell.

HELLO GOODBYE

One could argue that the truest assessment of a person's character is the manner in which they say goodbye. Goodbyes could be a part of life's greatest magic trick—we wait for the ones cared for to reappear and reveal to us how they did it.

These days I am no longer fazed when people exit my life. My last request is that they do not slam the door behind them when leaving. Maybe if our partners had front row seats to our past, they would see that we fought like hell to get here also. Instead they flee through back doors without respecting the time shared. They forget that couples are greater than their ending. There are times you will have to gain closure without hearing a goodbye. Closure for me never came tied to farewell; it began the moment I was willing to accept it.

THE MOTIONS

I miss her horribly, gravely, with all things evil. I miss her voice interrupting the silence—one touch gave feelings a reason to show face. Most of all, I miss *me* when with her. Her fragrance which once lingered on pillow tops and sheet bottoms is now fading. Sleeping no longer comes easy. I reach for her like spirited lilacs extending towards a sunlight hidden behind the kitchen shade. We embrace behind closed eyes and daydreams. As part of the unlucky, feelings for me aren't emotions—they are a loved one.

CLEAN HOUSE

Loving you became a cycle; clean myself up, get done dirty, soak in tears, rinse, dry eyes . . . repeat. Hurt starts with a heart sink then faucet drips. Emotions do not pour until you realize it is you left to wash dishes. We made the mess. This is our home. Your shirt is clean; why am I cleaning alone?

SOLO

If dating is practice for marriage, my failing relationships are prepping me for a lifetime of single. Hello and goodbye are in a footrace for my attention and always seem to tie. With reason, either I am transparent and vulnerable, or guarded with insecurity scanning IDs. I fear another hello's arrival and departure. I fear my growing preference in flying alone. I am aging out of hope and despite how many rights I write, Karma will not let me be. I have given her too many promises to keep.

UNTIMELY

At half past three,
or maybe a quarter to seven.
It could be Monday's summer evening
or during fall's brisk morn.
Everyone is saying,
"Be patient!
Love will find you at the right time."
I agree,
but when?

LATE NIGHT

I am not the wish upon a star type.
If you find me wide-awake
around 3 a.m.,
chances are I am heartbroken,
wishing whoever is on my mind
returns to let me sleep.

THE RANT

With the same eyes I have used to open myself up to new horizons, I have cried enough tears to build them. As relationships leave shore, I stand alone waving down their vacant decks. I am tired of jumping, too low to fall, too scared to get up, too angry to pray, and too insecure to believe things will get better. I find it interesting how men bear the names of players but the game often feels designed by a woman.

Men hurt in silence. The majority will leap into beds rather than landing in their feelings. If men communicated, would society notice both genders are greedy when it is time to eat? This cannot continue. If 15-year-old me had a bird's-eye view of my current love life, he would be disappointed. He might as well skip a few more decades because joy in love isn't arriving anytime soon.

The Rant. Maybe one day I will recognize this was the moment I had to say goodbye to you to say hello to her. I refuse to go back to who I was, I am content with me now, and confident in the man I will be tomorrow. I deserve amazing but still question. If not now—when? If not you—who?

TERRIBLE TOOS

Too many men behaving like babies; to mature is harder than aging.

Too many excuses for why men remain elusive.

Too many women rest their hearts with a body they should have never slept with.

Too much anger lies with the one she decided to keep.

Too many sisters are seeking a brother like her father while resistant to being anything like mom.

Too many women fail to realize daddy was like him until he had her.

Too many men refusing to man up leave women in a position where *they* have to.

Too often we forget wisdom comes with age and we aren't as smart as we think.

Too often we say goodbye once to say hello twice.

Too often when we want a second chance, it is too late. As adults, we face our own infantile behavior. We relive our own version of the terrible toos.

PILLOW TALK

She made me believe
this bed
was made for two.
Tonight my pillow whispered,
"It's ok. I miss her too."

HABITS

I am not superstitious.
Never believed in monsters
hiding behind closed doors
or under my bed,
but she could not sleep
until every door and drawer
was shut.
Even though she is no longer here,
before I rest my eyes,
I never forget
to check the closet.

DETENTION

I am in a relationship with a loved one behaving as if she doesn't think of me the same; living in a home that no longer feels like one. Every morning, beyond the curtain and a windowpane's gray, there is a future wanting to make introductions.

I glance into the dating pool but it is shallow—not because of the depth of the water, but because of the depth of its people. Staying home, albeit agonizing, is familiar, and familiar is safe. This love is stretching me until torn. I love her too much to leave because I don't love myself enough to go.

EXs AND WHYs

If a formula for finding love and getting over breakups existed, the majority would study just enough to pass the test. Finding love is immediate for some but moves at snail's pace for others. Those traumatized from wearing their hearts on their sleeves travel with caution after bumping it into the wrong people. People have a habit of falling out of love faster than the time it took to fall in, and an apology is not sufficient enough for the person who was hesitant to enter to begin with.

If it takes all of your strength to hold a relationship together, it will take all of your might to let it go. Cutting ties forces us to disconnect from the attachment; we slice pieces of ourselves when doing so. There is no time limit when parting ways. Recently broken up can mean three hours, three days, three months, and in some cases three years. Depending on the connection, no matter time and distance, it may feel as if that person were there three seconds ago.

Breakups take a portion of your confidence with it. Rejection tricks us into thinking the opinion of one aligns with rest of the world. It is not the case. You are still wanted, desired and needed. As confidence trickles back until you become whole again, it becomes the best part in your healing—realizing the world you thought ended, still exists. It was waiting patiently to deliver you someone better.

NO REWINDS

There are two types of people entering relationships: those who believe they have time and others moving with urgency. I loved the one who failed to support the latter. Why would you continue to let me fall knowing you were climbing out? Even though I am thankful for our moments, goodbye made me bitter. If possible, I would gift you all of our memories if in return, you could gift me back the time. It is the time lost that leads to resentment. Time is the one thing prayed for that is out of God's hands.

BEFORE I SAY GOODBYE

With farewells, for a moment we lose both love and sanity. We forget the pain felt, unlike memories, is never permanent. Goodbyes are tough because we move out with more than we moved in. We shed tears leaving the same person who made us cry more when together.

I have a habit of clinging to moments before the fall: pre, I love you—pre, I don't want to do this anymore. I am the staple barely holding our pages together. Those who know our story skimmed through, but we wrote it letter by letter, chapter by chapter, and it was us flipping its pages. It is hard closing the book of a love story when certain you penned the wrong ending.

When your heart is big and your love is heavy, most people cannot handle the weight. I had to release those weighing me down and accept some people do not care to fly. I can no longer want this for us. The words fall short, and my two cents aren't enough to create change. In time, you will learn the hard way. Isn't that how we learn to love the right way?

GUILTY

Your honor, her honor is all I care about. I have no suited soldier sharing opening remarks on my behalf. If loving her is criminal, find me guilty. I confess to stealing her heart without regret, kissing her until she suffocated, and killing her with kindness. Place her friends posing as jurors on trial; they have murdered this relationship more than we have.

SAD REALITY

My brain is a realist, my heart is an optimist,
and I struggle to get the two to negotiate.
—J. WESLEY

We give love chances, many chances, too many chances. We hope with each do-over we do better. We walk in broken relationships believing that once we reach the tunnel's end it will all make sense. We have to accept that we are the light, they are the tunnel, and we will be walking forever. Moving on is mentally a huge leap but baby steps away. We are not defined by the reasons people leave us. The baggage is their burden to carry. It was never ours to keep.

VACANCY

Broken hearts
are nothing more than
vacant homes
with a door slightly cracked
for the right one
to enter.

DORMANT

There is a difference between a weak man and a man who is only weak for you. Beast by nature—a gentleman by choice. Loving you never freed the animal. It quelled him. In order for us to survive, I believed the gentleman should overshadow the animal. I was wrong. I was so afraid of losing you, I lost myself attempting to please you. I did not lead, speak, command, as I should have. My fear of making a mess cheated you out of getting to know the real me. I am beast and gentleman. You needed to see the two. You needed to love them both.

THE DESTINED

Not all goodbyes are forever—those who call its name must endure living out the days until they find out. There are times when two must separate out of necessity. Distance, however far it may be, cannot keep two souls destined for one another apart. In these cases, each footstep taken when walking away brings them closer to meeting again.

PARDONED

Every day I wake hoping to forgive you.
Every night I pray tomorrow will be the day.
—J. WESLEY

Forgiveness rests within the pause before I remember; attached to emotions I thought eternally faded, vivid as the first day we met. Whether applied to acts or people, I shared it sparingly. I rather forget instead of forcing myself to apply the two.

Forgiving an ex came when it was needed . . . not wanted. Ironically, it never arrived when single. It slips into my life, bundled, in the form of someone better.

PART TWO
THE SWAY

———

Write his wrongs: plural. I wronged so many, been the one to so many, still the one to too many. Am I the one who got away or the reason she should have faith in a divine power that saved her from me?

I have broken many hearts to fix mine. What does the future hold? Will anyone be there holding me? Someone told me I raised the bar so high no woman will reach it. The bar marks the spot for her pedestal. I am not here to give pieces of me to every woman; my all belongs to one. My love is deep; some drown, others learn to swim—I cannot rescue them both.

ASCENSION

One of my biggest flaws is my ability to see
red flags in people from a distance but continue
to travel towards them and develop this closeness,
because I had to make sure the color was real.

—J. WESLEY

We settle with people who can spell love but cannot tell you what it means. Many want to reap the benefits but are unwilling to sow its fields. The selfish can never be a partner's better half. A power couple takes two.

Love is not a trinket shown off to friends. It is absent of worth, but valued. It is neither rich nor poor but can make one feel the two. Most come to know love when they cared for a person at their worst, forgave the unthinkable, and found themselves in a position where they received nothing and gave everything.

Throwing a jab or two is not fighting for love. To fight means to lay it all on the line. When all energy, hopes and wants are exhausted, you will yourself to fight again. Loving someone can wring you dry of emotions. When you believe it impossible to shed another tear, one moment can birth some anew. Love is flawed, sacrificed, scarred, and complex—it is hope, fulfillment, and joy. The reason people continue to fall in love after losing it is simple. Love hurts upon landing but it is the shit when you rise.

GUILTY PRAYERS

It is not that I forget to pray.
Sometimes I am too ashamed
to speak your name,
asking for forgiveness
when I don't seek change.
I do not want to waste your time.
It is bad enough
how much I waste mine.

LOVE'S ESCAPE

I have to let you go.
It pains me to clip your wings
knowing you dream of flight.
What I want
is the best for you
and hopefully,
somewhere between the rest
of the prayer asked and received,
best will return you to me.

REVERSE

The breakup affected us differently. Naivety made her experience emotionally, foreign to me. One day, karma delivered a pain straight to my doorway unlike anything felt before. I could not relate until I endured the same fate. To lose the one you swore was meant to stay is gut wrenching.

Prone to fixing whatever is broken, the majority of men are not strong enough to cope with heartbreaks. Whoever believed there was nothing worse than a woman scorned must not have met the man scorned by that same woman. Many men fail to try because they are afraid to fail. In return, women spoon-feed their love to men with little to no appetite. Do understand that anything you have ever lost was never meant to stay. If a flower can bloom from the concrete, any brute with a will to fight can grow to love.

LEARNING CURVES

As a man it might not be in my nature to nurture you. Boys are taught to rise to their feet after falling—march until the pain fades. We played sports and fought for recreation—daydreamed about having superpowers one day. Inside pillowed arenas, we imitated gladiators such as the Great Dad and Mighty Uncle who brought honor to our households. We mimicked them until we drank with them. Men provide. Hunters do not cry nor do they feel sorry for themselves when hands are bare. Hunters. Keep. Hunting. Growing up we learned how to provide for a tribe but overlooked the details on how nurture one. Now an adult, when she asked me to be more sensitive, I couldn't. It wasn't because I didn't want to . . . I didn't know how.

SLEEP'S SHELTER

In passing, guests notice the markings of stubborn hinges refusing to let go. Overheard are the whispers of a revolving door that no longer dwells here. When younger, meaningless sex was a reflection of my partner. I grew up and it became evident that it was a reflection of my character.

My bedroom is greater than a playground for adults who only speak during recess. It is where life receives its first chance, sins are forgiven, and my Lord and I speak the most. Whether I am in your safekeeping or you are my safe haven, you protect me. My respect for you and myself has grown. This is why I am selective with whom I bring into your space.

PRIDE AND EGO

L ove does not elude us as often as we think. It is my belief that pride and ego confuse our inability to get things right with our refusal to make things better. Pride in excess, like a bruised ego, can turn an apology into silence. We understand no one is perfect, but pride is often unforgiving. Pride expects blessings from sinners but gets upset when they sin. An ego's actions will speak for itself when the brain is stubborn and the mouth is silent.

Do not let your ego control your decisions; force it to accept no one is without flaws. Take pride in giving your all. If your hands are not equipped, either you learn how to use the tools or respect that you are not the right one for the job. Take pride in the journey. Be proud of who you are. Be prideful, not ego-filled.

THE DOUBLE STANDARD

Did you think hiding behind a double standard would keep you safe? Newsflash, men are hoes too. Hearing tales of men swift to move on and reluctant to move in grows tiresome. Insecure men spread themselves among multiple women to feel whole. While accruing notches in your belt, what good is it when unable to wear the pants in your household? If men frowned upon whoring more than they glorified it, trust and relationships would be stronger. Staying devoted to a woman doesn't make you weak; it makes you a man.

What if the one labeled a hoe fell for every person she slept with? Perhaps the partners she saw futures with blurred her vision. If they brought something to the table and lost their appetites, would you still label her? Could you still label her? She let them in; they let themselves out. Is it fair to mock her? Why not call her courageous for trying again? No, she didn't wait for marriage. Did you?

THE PREREQUISITES

Her man must be a provider, protector, and soldier. He must be sensitive, and spontaneous with homebody qualities. When intimate, the lack of dominance and willingness to release control are deal-breakers. His dress-wear must consist of tailored suits and the casual trendy. It is essential that he is intelligent with a touch of hood, and able to impress parents, friends, and social media acquaintances. She says she wants a man—not once did she mention the woman she will be.

CAST AWAY

A leaf will remove itself from tree's embrace to waltz with single friends in the grass. When time to return to its perch, no matter how much an oak wants to lift it up, it cannot.

None of them were around to witness me mourn her departure. I alone felt the spots she kept warm turn frigid. Falling asleep feeling worthless, waking up unwanted, was a vicious cycle; the hurt clutched me until numb. When she returned with friends in tow willing to boost her, I had no branches to lower. Her friends made it seem like being single was the thing to be. Enjoyed for a moment, it proves temptation can lead you away but it can't always return you home.

THE UPGRADE

Convinced her best was not me—she passed up good searching for perfect. I collected my emotions off the floor, lifted my head, and walked towards a future without her. My confidence is shaken but my pride remained intact. It will be ok. I don't compete for spots. I am the spot.

My light will dim and flicker longer than it should but once I am turned off you cannot turn me back on. What seemed quick to her was an eternity to me. I did not answer the calls nor the knocks at my door. I had to let her go; my heart was too heavy to save us both.

THE UNHEARD

The louder her voice rises, I can tell the tune she sings is not about me. A minor argument snowballed into something greater, with our words refusing to shake hands tonight. My pride is hurt, so is my woman, and I am stuck trying to figure out who needs saving the most.

We have been through it before. He is not me, she is not her, we are not them and they are not us. Hearing her greet me as every ex who exited her doors makes me want to leave. I can't be the blessing paying for another man's sins. She needs to let them go, before I do.

FOREVER

If I wished for timing to get us right, would God's clock need adjusting or only our own? We accepted fate brought us together; why can't we accept that fate is tearing us apart? Do you want me for a moment or a lifetime? I deserve a consistent kind of happy. I deserve someone who sees my flaws as a reason to stay, not leave, because they come attached to everything that is good about me. These days when you push me away I leave another piece of me there. The route has grown more familiar than you.

EVICTION

Are you afraid to fall in love?
No. Experience has proven, loving a person will never guarantee its return in equal measure. When I love, I am vulnerability resting in the comfort of someone I trust. See, I am not afraid to fall. I fear when I do, the host will ask me to leave.

KEEP SEARCHING

I am not the perfect solution,
only the sole answer
to a special problem.
My drawback is
at times
I get tired from jumping from
equation to equation
to see where I fit in.
Maybe love
is both sides of a coin
meant to be called in the air,
and if doesn't land in your favor
flip again.

DISCERNMENT

You know.
You know when there is potential—
you know when it is real.
You know when it is fading,
and you know when it is gone.
You know it's a rebound to forget what you lost—
you know you can do better than the one that you have.
You know when you messed up a good thing—
you know when you are too embarrassed to show face.
You know when you are afraid to start over—
you know when you are trapped where you stand.
You know you want to search until you find it—
you know when you don't know what you want.
You know when the best thing to do is walk away—
you know that you will hurt them more if you stay.
They may not know because you choose to remain silent,
but the conversation was had with yourself,
and you know.

HISTORICALLY SPEAKING

She wants more but I have nothing more to give her. I am the man old flames longed for me to be. What was potential to them, I made tangible for her. She does not know how far I have come because she only knows me from the time I arrived. In time I will get to the place she pictured but history has proven that she will not be around to see it.

THREAD LIGHTLY

I am a bunch of flaws
stitched together,
hoping my partner
cares enough
to not pull the seams
when attempting
to reach for me.

BODY LANGUAGE

I don't talk. I do. My problem is that my love is shown more than heard. Simple winks prove one eye is willing to miss you but the other does not have the strength to let you go. Kisses while you are sleeping whisper *I love you* in your dreams. When I hold you tighter, stare deeper, and stroke your hair, that is me speaking a language I pray you comprehend.

VOICELESS

I witness descendants
of Queens,
mute their beauty
with modern songs,
then ask that I
fall in love with lyrics,
I will never sing.

DEAR J.

If said, would you have returned the favor? Neither of us intended on being here. Where would we go after? What was felt: deeper than kisses, greater than sex. We felt the same, but knew once spoken everything would change. Our biggest lie was telling ourselves that neither of us would catch feelings. We were never supposed to be here. If I told you that I love you, where would we go from there?

DESTINATION US

Her fix in a moment's kiss keeps her high in low situations. She is hurt. Her shirt is clean but emotionally she has been trampled on. Whether men step up or step down she is the one stepped over.

She cried with purpose. She watered her seed long enough to blossom into the woman she needed to be. Deeply rooted, she pursued her light and learned to rise above it all. She is special. Her thorns only prick those pricks too selfish to hold her the way she needs to be held.

He doesn't do drugs—he does love—that's worse. He is weary. Illiterate, he fails miserably at reading between the lines. He feels dumb when he cannot find the words to say. He is deprived; starving for a healthy relationship for so long you can see his ribs.

Those who fall in love the hardest take the longest to rise. These two are traveling separate paths leading to the same destination. Whether it is once upon a time or happily ever after, these two will meet and they have a story to tell.

DISTANT VISIONS

I didn't see her for who she was. I saw her for what she could be. I saw strength behind a teardrop. I saw power take the backseat when she felt weak. I saw a job leading to a career with her taking the lead. Every time I saw a future—I saw me. I saw flaws as a part of the total package I wanted to unwrap every day. I saw that none of this mattered because she did not see it the same way.

ALL GROWN UP

Countless women slipped through these fingertips. Losing grasp taught me two things: the importance of prayer and how to keep a firmer grip. I stopped letting fear get the best of me to allow her to get the best me. I did the uncomfortable—traveled outside of my comfort zone and discovered her standing there.

Communication has always been my struggle. It took a woman's love to make me want to fix me. If I cannot speak it, I write it, and if I run out of paper, I act it out.

When loving someone, one must respect a partner's boundaries. I am learning how to be close but not suffocate and give space without becoming distant. Being a couple must never stunt the growth in becoming stronger individuals. A better her, coupled with a better me, creates a better us.

Love with conviction, not out of convenience. Appreciating a woman for her flaws gives a man more of her to love. Too busy is for those on the bottom of the priority list. I make time, carve time, share time, reserve time, and lose sleep if needed to spend seconds, even a few, with you. I have you now—I get it now—I am all grown up now.

HER WORTH

No scale can measure a woman's worth. She is the first rite of passage every king must find his way through. No matter how powerful he grows, it was mom who gave him strength. She is the foundation, pillar, and shelter—a rock with a soft spot. Without her, there is no him. We caused women enough pain entering this world to turn around and disrespect them.

HER

She is as frightened as she is courageous; built with an uncanny ability to camouflage nervousness with composure. Not the most vocal in the room, she will leave with the award for most observant. She appreciates the beauty in others but at times is so blinded by her flaws that she forgets to acknowledge her own. Her skill is the ability to hope when centered in crisis and dream amidst nightmares. She has given up, given in, given her all, and mustered up the courage to try again—all in the spirit of a love hesitant in answering her prayers. She walks without struggle, moves towards purpose. She never claimed to be perfect; she too is working on getting it right.

CONCEALED

When a man wants you, you will know; when he doesn't you will question. Too many relationships teeter between privacy and secrecy. What is done as a couple is private; who you are with must never be kept secret. A partner should not have to stand next to you in order for the world to know who they are. My spirit breaks for those lingering in the darkness waiting for a spotlight to shine. Time will pass along with opportunities. In order to realize two people are on the same page, someone needs to speak up.

TRAVELS

I am somewhere between
mother's darling boy
and an in-law's future son.
While I travel along life's lonely way,
I extend my arms with hope
that I am within reach to feel both.

THE OTHERS

There is beauty in the broken; to her I was gorgeous. For years I resisted giving my heart away, and one Tuesday, I found it safe in the hands of the delicate. She grew to care for mine more than hers.

When a man changes for the better it is not done because of what she said; he will do it because of who she is. When a man fears losing his woman more than change, he will change.

Men are out there running from relationships as if a woman who loves you is not the best thing to come home to. If they knew what true love felt like, it would be sought not evaded. I have seen many bright women moved to tears over shady men and because of this, I refuse to be the reason she runs to him over me. When you break your woman's heart you also break yours. A man should love his woman like there is no tomorrow, wake up and do it again.

BITTER SWEET

She is happy I grew up,
pleased with my moving on,
and notices I am the man
she believed I could be.
Within the shadow of her voice
masked by words said,
I can hear her heart whisper,
"Why couldn't you be this man for me?"

SELFLESS

I cannot help
that I am a giver
born to serve,
but even I have moments
when I need to be fed.
When you live a life
placing the needs of others
before your own,
the day you put yourself first
feels selfish.
It's not.
It is your turn.
It was always your turn.

IMPERFECT TIMING

Sometimes the hardest part of being a great catch is accepting not everyone's hands are strong enough to hold you. People will drive you into the arms of another rather than building the strength to carry you on their own. In lessons of the heart we convince ourselves that the greater the struggle the greater the promised land and journey with partners we were never meant to settle with.

When forced to learn lessons in love from substitute teachers, it takes a different kind of person to provide a different type of love. I was there to witness her descent—I caught her before she hit rock bottom. Her ex never expected her to fall into the arms of the man strong and smart enough to not let her go. Holding her has been more rewarding than catching her. He was not ready but I was prepared. Until a man can look beyond the surface of a woman, he will never know the difference between pretty and beautiful.

LOVE SEASON

Those who speak of love only as rose petals and shining suns must not have experienced its many seasons. Relationships are autumn leaves too stubborn to change colors and a cold shoulder's brutal winter. Love will scorch those too comfortable under a summer glow and drench others caught beneath spring clouds too emotional to stop weeping. Love blossoms, fades, withers, and endures. True love, no matter the climate, will always find a way to adjust.

THE CONCERT

Not once have I listened
to the faint music
of a woman's tears
and applauded her song.
I never caught its beat—
could not comprehend the lyrics—
but I did connect to its melody.
From my seat,
either I
gave her reason to leave the stage,
or allowed my tears
to sing along.

PERFECTION

Who are you perfection? Are you noun? Verb? An adjective used to describe a horizon too narcissistic to greet anyone? I lost partners—good partners—in search of you. An assembly of personalities left lesson plans, portfolios, and stethoscopes joining me to get to you. The lone item hauled back was a lesson learned. Relationships are doomed from the onset when aiming for perfection; perfection keeps walking away.

THE PASSAGE

The honeymoon phase is wonderful but a relationship does not begin until it reaches the land of comfort and familiarity. These grounds, where two become one, and change is difficult no matter how much you cherish them. What is cute, in excess, can become annoyance, and the closeness of settling down forever is as much a reality as it is frightening.

Is it worth it? Yes! Falling in love allows you to fall in love with yourself during the process. A couple, when familiar, must not become complacent. Partners must surrender to love in full because there is no room to love in halves or quarters. It will bring the two to higher heights. Fall in love—fall down if you have to, but make sure you rise in it.

SCALES

It is interesting
how one can confuse love for sex.
Love is greater,
lasts longer,
and defined after the act.
Love is the comfort between two
in a bedroom
similar to plush pillows,
soft linens,
and an excused bathroom break
around 3 a.m.

BEYOND FENCES

Perhaps the grass is greener to test the strength of our relationship while disguised as the fence. It was here our picnics brought loved ones together. We dashed across it in excitement to see one another. We left our dirt at the doorstep, entered and kissed stress goodbye. Maintaining this home was not easy, but worth it. The neighbors yard will always look greener—none of them have a history like we do.

SOUL GUARDIAN

I don't leave memories.
I leave traces.
If I loved you,
I touched you—
hands, heart and spirit.
If anyone can reach that deep,
maybe they belong there.
But,
in order for them to feel your love,
and enter your heart,
they will have to pass me
to meet you.

PROTECTOR PROTECT HER

I will protect my heart
at any cost
and do so twice as hard
after giving it to her.
If she is cut
I am torn.
When she cries,
I suffer.
I stand in front
when she needs shielding,
and I always have her back.
If any man tries to bring harm
to my woman,
this ain't a fist fight—
it is war.

SEE YOU WHEN I GET THERE

I would have moved faster—given goodbyes sooner—cried shorter—thanked God longer. When saying it will be ok, I would have meant it. Drinks to forget endings would have been toasts to new beginnings. I would have and more if I knew you were waiting for me around the corner.

If you are too good to be true—lie to me forever. Relationships were never my priority. To a certain degree, it amazes me how quickly I gave up those associates as a bachelor to master you.

Lifting you up does not make you weaker; it makes us stronger. It gives us balance. If the weight of this world should bear heavy on your shoulders, let me stand in your stead. Do not worry if my head shivers by the Arctic and I lose footing as the Pacific leaks; the weight pales in comparison to seeing you with a heavy heart.

You make forever seem temporary. May our feelings never alter upon leaving the altar. Whatever is breaking you down is preparing you for me. One day, we will meet in the same room, at the same time and call it home. Until then, my comfort is in knowing that you are out there looking for me—somewhere around the corner.

THE MOMENT

The moment: a mystical place where a hello can flourish and blurted words injure possibilities between two. Apologies are often late on arrival, or accompanied by pride, who is notorious for ruining the show. The moment is a scenic route with the ability to take anyone off-road. What is said can be forgiven not forgotten, and the tone chosen, can drown out the words. When you find yourself at the moment, think before you act. You can lose people, by losing yourself, in the moment.

NO GOOD MEN

Good men exist and women ruin relationships also. Many good men are indoors with the one who saw a future with him when others didn't. He also has himself to blame. He masked his desire to be her man behind a friendship he hoped would lead to more. Nevertheless, too often women overlook the man who didn't fit the bill to eventually lose hope in a dime who will never change. One is who she wanted; the other is who she needed.

Why do fading relationships marry the notion that little is better than nothing? She barely speaks because he hardly listens. I have seen too many women lose their senses while waiting for a man to come to his. This may not be you, but most of us know her. Eventually this relationship will end, not because she wants it to but because it has to.

"Chivalry no longer exists!" Hearing this from repeat offenders seeking courtship becomes tiresome. As adults, we know the difference between right and wrong; sometimes we do not care. How many nights must women lay with a man to realize that they are not a star? Love does not surround you with riches—it fills you with it.

As men, we must take responsibility for our actions. We need to stop leading women towards futures and abandoning them in the present. While she journeys across our desert, we create mirages that vanish the moment she arrives. Most women are not thirsty for men—they are parched from being with them.

When dating, you will take a few steps with some, walk miles with others, and travel the distance with one. Remaining optimistic while navigating the three is a daunting task. Though many have left, better is coming. It was always on its way, even when you lost yours.

100

She made 100 mistakes. I matched them with 100 acts of forgiveness, which created 100 learning opportunities for the two of us. She attempted to apologize 100 times but I would not allow it. She was sincere the first time; I didn't need to hear it more than once. I have surpassed 100 attempts to forget, and yes, she has given me 100 reasons to leave, but I love her and that is enough for me to stay. Many believe I gave her too many chances. To me, she is worth 100 more.

ACCESS GRANTED

Her heart is home.
One day fear locked me out.
She refused to speak,
and wouldn't let me in.
I grabbed her shoulders,
pulled her close,
and told her,
"I am yours until heaven calls me back."
She shed a tear,
looked into my eyes,
then I slowly climbed back
through her windows.

DELIVER ME

L ord, send me a good woman." He did. I messed it up. Months later I asked, "Forgive me Lord; please send me a good woman." He listened. I failed to do my part. One night I pleaded, "I cannot do this alone Lord. Mold me into the man I need to be in order to care for a good woman. Send me a woman whose spirit runs so strong, when I touch her I touch you Lord." He listened and granted. This time I was ready.

UPWARD BOUND

I rather open the spirits in people than pop bottles. In this lifetime I may not be viewed as cool or someone in style, but the day I approach heaven's gates my efforts will make me V.I.P. When I walk along its gloried path, dirtied with a crooked halo, let it be proof that some work harder than others to get here.

FOUR

When you meet the one there will be no
trumpets playing and angels singing. It is you,
with your conscience telling you this one is different
and urging you to not mess it up.
—J. WESLEY

Relationships never claimed top expression on the totem pole. I never stumbled across a glass slipper to return to a princess while returning home from work. When asked, "How did you know she was the one?" I didn't.

Looking back, I remember what she wore down to the colors in each pattern. I can pencil the angle her head tilted as the sun first held her cheek. At that moment, I did not know if she was the one but I knew without a doubt that she was special. The closer I got, the more emotions stirred within. I could feel in my soul, that in another lifetime, I loved this woman before.

PART THREE
LOVE NOTES

———

A relationship consists of two individuals responsible for the safekeeping of one another. Love in its purest form requires a shared mindset by those who care enough to ask, "What are we willing to do for us?" The answer, whether a Sunday morning or a Thursday's noon, must always be, "Whatever it takes."

THE REASONS

Love is why waves hurry ashore reaching for sand too stubborn to abandon home. It is in the captain's journey toward a horizon he will never meet and why she stares in return wondering if her ship will ever get there. Love is the calm before and after storms throw tantrums. Love's chosen party must brave its waters. With reason, no one is strong enough to swim its current alone—we sink until the bottom is met. Then it consumes you. Until you drown in love my friend, you have never lived.

HOOKED

You are first thought
during morning rise,
and last
before night rest.
Either I am in love
or I am in trouble.

SUPERSTITION

I never believed in
love at first sight,
so I blinked twice
because at first glance
my heart knew
it was you.

PICTURE THIS

She has a smile that could make a stutterer say his name right, and remains true to herself without apology. She has no desire to be molded-only felt. With care, these hands have traced her from crown to foot bottoms. While studying her shape, I mastered her curves. I cannot draw. I cannot paint. But I do know art.

THE CALLING

Why do you love her?"

Good question. I never put much thought into it before. Why does the sun light the morning sky? Why does the moon tuck us in at night? Like them, I figured I was born with a job to do—mine happens to be fulfilling. I never let her pretty face fool me, I knew loving this woman would be work—so I rolled up my sleeves and came to get my hands dirty. I was created to love her. Life never gave me a choice.

RIGHTFUL ARMS

If you find another man who loves you more than me— tell your dad I said hello. If he asks, "What are your intentions for my daughter?" The response is, "Take the reins as if you never let go."

I did not come here to love you like you are ordinary. I am the reason exes never got it right. **I am here—I am now—I am tomorrow.** Let me take your breath away and stick around long enough to give it back. Whenever you breathe love, you will inhale exhale me.

This love is soul deep. Your heart is mine for the taking, but it will never be mine to keep; let me be the one it beats for. My words have to be the pulse delivering my messages. I need you to hear me. I have to be the veins.

MERGER

Falling in love
is deeper than anything physical,
easily proven in the stare shared by two souls
desperately wanting to be there.
They are not only looking,
but speaking,
and a pupil will teach you,
what is seen is more than a reflection.
When you see yourself,
it is proof
that a part of you,
lives in there.

QUESTIONS

Can I protect you from all things possible?
Can I be your comfort when things are beyond our control?

Can I make love to your mind first and watch you birth the thought of a better us?

Can I be the promise never broken or the bond that never loses grip?

Can I listen when you are silent because that is when you are saying the most?

Can I be the one you never imagined having but deep down knew you deserved?

Can I?

ANNA MAY

When the moment of intimacy arrived, she wept. I attempted to stop; she gripped me tighter, drew me closer while holding a look as if she felt me before. One stare, made it clear that it was not the feeling, but her feelings leading to tears. For the first time in my life, I knew what it felt like to be the piece making a woman complete.

ARTISTRY

Our bedroom is where we share our artistry. We are . . . two pieces too abstract for others to make out. Our blend creates colors rainbows dream of and shadows long to be. Within a muddled world fixated on black and white, we find amusement amidst its gray. She models a beauty I can never master but attempt to anyway. Our bed is our canvas. With each stroke, we paint.

WARNING

Last night she had a nightmare.
I did not wake her;
instead, I kissed her forehead,
sending a warning to whatever
disturbing her
that they do not want me
to come in there.

LOVE, DRIVING, PIANO

You are the driving force behind this heartbeat. Relentless, while trapped in confusion, it lunges forward attempting to leave home, and is yanked back as a reminder that he is not tied to you-it's mine. Lunge, come back . . . beat . . . beat . . . beat. Love has taught me that hearts are jealous because emotions are fleeting—traveling to places, bodies, and settling in locations it will never see. Reminiscent to the piano, audiences rarely experience tickling its keys, but fall in love with the belted melodies more than their source. My love will never cease reaching for you— intensifying when you are near, because my heart lies still with me, but it beats for you.

COMFORT

As morning first peered through my window shade, I caught a glimpse of my love resting naked. She was bare of clothes and makeup, stripped of lies and truth. Without waking her, I held her hand, kissed her think, and wrapped my arms around her—touching her skin-to-skin—holding her soul to soul.

MRS. WRITE

I started writing you a love letter—damaged my desk in the process because what needed to be said could not be contained within the margins of this paper. I entered this hoping we would be each other's last—you know, last first kiss, last first date. When I listened to your story, I knew I wanted to be more than a character in the next chapter. I had to be the cover holding you together—I needed to be the one protecting your pages from being ripped.

We cuddle for different reasons: I keep you warm; you keep me whole. Confession: I am not a morning person. I have energy while the sun yawns because I am a *you* person.

Your first name paired with my last will be my greatest poem penned. You, the lyrics to my favorite song; I, an amateur singer thank God I can hold your note. Your praises sung until my voice is lost-resurrected in my hum. I cannot give you perfect. What I will do is give you all of my broken pieces and hope when placed in your arms, we will weigh the same.

DREAM CATCHER

I stood guard as my chest played pillow and counted. One, three, seven blinks—then she fell asleep. Kissed her forehead and whispered, "I'll see you in five."

I am not the man of her dreams but she is the woman in mine. In there our stories are different. She, the princess of the ball, and me, too poor to cross the castle doors. I never swam the moat, nor did I storm the gates. In this story, I am not the knight in shining armor; just a man atop a lone hill holding his love in thought while watching his royalty tango from afar.

Nothing beats having the woman of your dreams and the woman you wake next to, be the same person. I give that man posted on his hill a chance. Every day I kiss her lips as if I am writing our names in the sand, and then do my part to make sure her tide never washes away what I worked for. Not only am I blessed to live the dream—I am loving her.

DESTINED

I love you. What was lower than a whisper alarmed the heavens. My angels sounded their trumpets and rejoiced. They saw me growing, knew she was coming, and waited until the two paths crossed. Those three words startled the devil out of his sleep. He will do everything in his power to turn love into hate and bring this to an end. He won't. Together we stand in prayer—we will not fall victim to sin.

PICTURE PERFECT

Relationships are pieces of art openly displayed for the world to interpret. Our blues almost sunk us. There were times we lost touch of why we started. When distant, love kept us close. Our mistakes, those smears, did not make us horrible—it made us human. Something about us attracts audiences near and far. They marvel at our life within the frame. We did not understand initially, but later learned that love can be flawed. We do not have to be picture perfect to create a perfect picture.

WHETHER OR NOT

At times, she is unpredictable—
some weekdays storm clouds,
most weeks sunshine.
No matter the weather,
I love her the same.
I have learned to
dress light when needed
and appreciate her beauty
when she rains.

THE LAY

There is a deeper side to intimacy.
It is where one can lay their vulnerability
next to another without worry.
It requires connection without touch—
love without words—
harmony without sound.
This closeness
explores a depth well beyond the surface.
It is connection through separation—
two heartbeats—one pulse.
We have this type of intimacy,
and when I ask her to "sleep with me"
I am not talking about sex.

FOR YOU I WILL

Failed attempts with relationships left us believing we were nothing more than the match lit. Together we chose to be the flame. Lighting her fire isn't difficult—keeping it lit is. Kisses before she crosses the door is my way of showing what is felt is not up for discussion. When she stares, I play mirror. It is neither scary nor creepy. That gaze is evidence this woman is madly in love and knows it. She glows whenever she sees me; I would be a fool to give her any reason to dim the light.

Part of loving a woman is learning how to read between her lines. When she wants one—I know when to purchase two. When something is off, I can tell when others don't. Love does not always give you the entire story; it forces you to use your imagination. And for you, I will.

REUNITED

My woman was not waiting on a rescue. You knew the only one who could save you was the one you prayed to. Those prayers lit my path until I reached your welcome mat; I came to call you home. I did not recognize your face, but the feeling was everything expected. I prayed so hard for you—I knew you before I met you. We are proof God listens and the universe plays favorites.

PRAYER REQUEST

If you ever
feel sudden warmth or chills,
it is because I send messages
in the form of prayer
and the blessings asked for
find you and cover.

INFERNO

As she lay naked comforting my comforter, there was certainty I would sin with a prayer answered. She is heaven-sent, straight to the devil's playground. We are two flames, fortunate to share one dance, showing the universe what cool looks like before burning the motherfucker down. The more we danced, the more we burned. We stood amid it all—fireproof. With each lift she torched heaven's hem and hell's crown. Ash and embers share tales in the wind of the two who made God and the Devil call truce. If loving this woman is a sin—heaven, I apologize.

WE ARE

I kissed her temple too many times to not know what she is thinking—held her palms too many times to not know what she holds dear. I traced her lips too many times to not know what love tastes like—slept with her too many times to not know dreams come true.

I am not the best man out there, but I am best at what I do. She loves that I pour my all into her in excess. There is no way of hiding what I feel, even when alone. When you see me, you see her, and if you listen carefully, you will hear us.

Our differences make our relationship enjoyable. She laughs uncontrollably at jokes I never get and dances to rhythms I can never catch. I drink darks—she loves lights. She enjoys quiet; I need noise to sleep at night. I walk with hands in pocket; she reaches for mine anyway. With interests laying on opposite sides of the track, one would believe that we would never work. A couple can be unalike in many ways; all they need in common is love.

MY TURN

I want you more than any other man who came before. I don't care to know their names or what they did. How they felt can't exceed how I feel. I want you like a baby wants to walk—like a robin wants to sing—like the hungry wants to be fed and the lost want to be found. If those men wanted you like I do—you wouldn't be here. I want you to stay here.

SOUL BEAUTY

I told her she is beautiful
and it has nothing to do
with her appearance.
By the time I finished
explaining myself,
her soul began to blush.

LOST AND FOUND

She took me to a place too secret for fingers to hold—where kisses are interpreted and whispers lay their crowns. Here, memories and dreams neighbor—today's sight gives way to tomorrow's vision. We watch moons tumble, suns leap, volcanoes calm tempers, and waterfalls dive into their tranquil. I know not the coordinates; I cannot pinpoint where I am. I found myself by losing myself in this woman. When together, we are anywhere we want to be.

JOIN ME

There is a major difference between her mirror and I: when she questions herself in my presence, my lips never hesitate to remove all doubt. It is simple: if your man is not your biggest fan, get another man. I refuse to let another support her dreams more than me. Whether she suffers from stage fright or delivers the performance chattered around town for weeks, my woman always receives a round of applause from me. As your man, I am here to love you, console you, hold you, defend you, mend you, and most importantly, wed you. I prayed for you, and God . . . sent . . . you.

Her journey in meeting me did not arrive free of bruises. I held her chin, leaned in and whispered, "Put your tears aside, you will not need them for a while." When walking away from those exes, she was moving in my direction, so I gave up parts of me to make room for her. I let go of who I was and gave in to the man I needed to be. She is not the type bragged about to friends, but the reward that makes a man bend knees, clasp hands and thank the higher power for listening.

SOLEIL

If I told you
how stunning she is,
my truest feelings would be
lost in translation.
She isn't the physical attraction
teens link to puppy love.
She need not be compared to
inanimate objects held dear.
She is Michelangelo's canvas,
Angelou's pen—
that type of special.
A rare form of beauty,
a unique version of love.

I SEE YOU

When I told her, "You are beautiful"
she didn't believe me. She said, "Look, my hair
isn't done, I'm not dressed up, and I don't have
my make-up on." I responded, "Exactly."
—J. WESLEY

I can see the light in your shadow and feel the sadness within a forced smile. If you knew how in love I am with the sound of your voice, you would never be silent again. When the world believes everything is ok, remember the three you can never fool: your God, your conscience, and me.

Give me your broken, fears, and unwanted. Hand me your past—let them see your future is here. Give me you: natural, raw, down to the roots, and I will reassure you that you are naturally beautiful. You cannot tell me that true beauty isn't natural.

YOUR FIRST MY LAST

What do I want from you?

    I don't want to be the one you settled with—I have to be the one you were searching for. I do not want you to catch me when I fall—I need you to make it with worth the trip. Elevate me. If it doesn't bring out the best in you then it isn't love. There is a difference between want and need—you have to be why I balance the two. I need to want you. I want to need you. When I say "I do" repeat after me. Allow the expression on my face to give honeymoons reason to love their job. I want to make love and take turns choosing a name. Be the reason my heart can tell my brain, "I told you so." What do I want? A future isn't a future if you are not in it. I want you.

FAMILY GATHERING

When I introduce you to mom, I am not seeking her approval. I am showing her that she raised a man wise enough to see special and bring her home. Sit at the table where she pulled our family together—where aunts held loving hands, grandma shared the stories of old, and cousins daydreamed about being there. Make yourself comfortable as we say grace, talk, and laugh. My family has class and you belong here. I want you to sit at our table.

BEFORE I SAY I DO

The sexiest piece she will
ever wear is my last name.
—J. WESLEY

I have learned in order to accomplish your goals, first you must write them. My love, please accept what is said as both confession and promise. I vow to uphold my vows every day, work diligently every day, and make you want to remarry me every day. We walk hand in hand, side by side, not because of who we are but because equal is what we are. You do not define me—you give me meaning. I only know what love is because I know who you are. Queen, you are the future bearer of royalty and the backbone of this kingdom; we do not stand unless you are upright. I vow the day I say I do—I will. No more secrets. This is how I feel. This is my confession.

You are everything in between once upon a time and happily ever after. Let me continue to be your knight in shining armor, even though for you I am selfish enough to keep you to myself as the village foe. We share a connection too strong to name love. Secretly love from my heart whispered to me, *I strive to be exactly what you two feel.*

Making me so in love with you is the love you exude. Time flies while lost in each other's eyes. When silent, if we listen closely we can hear our souls engaging in intimate conversation. That warm feeling I get must be from the candle lit. Your soul noticed some dark sections around my heart and thought it was appropriate.

What we have encompassed is the reason the majority get married and, for lack thereof, unfortunately, divorce. You understand me as if you were the one who named me. In return, I promise to hold you in the highest regard as my mother, yet humble myself as if I am in the presence of my father.

Treasured are the nights we spend together. I dream before dreaming, suffering from nightmares when I wake and you are not there. You give my butterflies, butterflies. Let me be the one to erase your pain, and if that proves too much, I'll catch every tear just so I can feel what you're going through.

Once limited to only consonants, you've introduced me to vowels such as *u* and *I*, expanding my horizon. With your help, I am able to formulate new words. Cohesively, we strive to become each other's punctuation. Adding an effect to one another's thinking, daily, allowing us to construct paragraphs monthly, creating yearly that which begins with once upon a time and ends with happily ever after. The story of our life.

ACKNOWLEDGMENTS

To my circle who believed me in me from day one—even through the periods I doubted myself. When I rise, you are coming with me. I will never forget.

Ashley: You spent countless nights being my editor, cheerleader, reality check but most importantly my friend. This book would not have gotten here without your help. Thank you.

Kasha: The only thing in return you asked for is that I produce the best I had. I did and you made it look spectacular. Thank you for the talks, the ideas and the design. You are proof that we meet everyone for a reason.

Twin: Thank you. You know what I mean within those two words.

ABOUT THE AUTHOR

J. Wesley penned his first love note in the third grade. His crush could not afford a stamp so she checked the "no" box and personally returned it. With that said, J. Wesley received his first heartbreak in the back of a Brooklyn third grade classroom. Decades later, he mustered up the courage to write again and became the voice behind Writehiswrongs.com. His following stretches out to multiple continents but never has his first heartbreak ever reached out to say she was sorry. I guess that is life.

Website: www.writehiswrongs.com
Instagram: writehiswrongs
Twitter: writehiswrongs
Tumblr: writehiswrongs
Etsy: writehiswrongs
Facebook: www.facebook.com/writehiswrongs